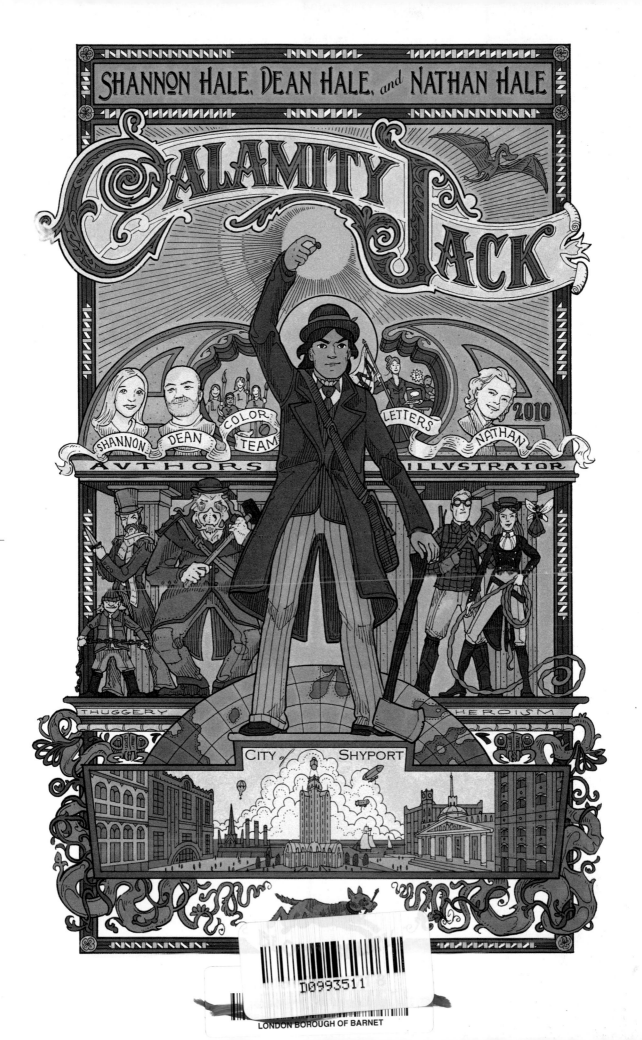

Also by Shannon Hale

RAPUNZEL'S REVENGE

THE BOOKS OF BAYERN
THE GOOSE GIRL
ENNA BURNING
RIVER SECRETS

PRINCESS ACADEMY

THE BOOK OF A THOUSAND DAYS

Bloomsbury Publishing, London, Berlin and New York

First published in Great Britain in 2010 by Bloomsbury Publishing Plc
36 Soho Square, London, W1D 3QY

A CIP catalogue record of this book is available from the British Library

ISBN 978 0 7475 8742 2

Printed in China by South China Printing Co Ltd

1 3 5 7 9 10 8 6 4 2

Book design by Nathan Hale
Balloons and lettering by Melinda Hale
HushHush and Pulp Fiction fonts by Comicraft
Colour mapping by Yodit Solomon, Melinda Hale, Lindsay Hale,
Layna Connors and Lauren Widtfeldt

All papers used by Bloomsbury Publishing are natural, recyclable products made from wood
grown in well-managed forests. The manufacturing processes conform to the environmental
regulations of the country of origin

www.bloomsbury.com/childrens
www.shannonhale.com

For Max and Maggie,
the best teammates a couple of schemers
could ever hope for.

—S. H. AND D. H.

To Greg, Riley, and Rebekah.
Three in-laws, three outlaws.

And with thanks to Shannon and Dean—
no relation, but a lot of admiration.

—N. J. H.

Part 1: The Beanstalk Bonanza

I think of myself as a criminal mastermind...

...with an unfortunate amount of bad luck.

I was born to scheme.

32 Jack

See? You can tell just by looking at me.

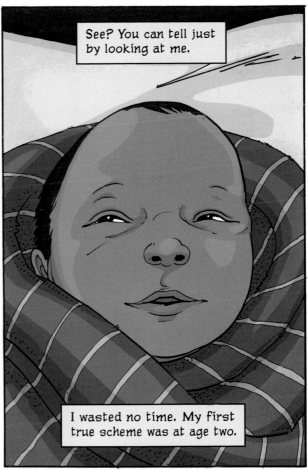

I wasted no time. My first true scheme was at age two.

Let's call it...

the Sugarbowl Plan

I'd see something I wanted...

...and my mind couldn't help figuring out how to get it.

My early years were measured by great plans...

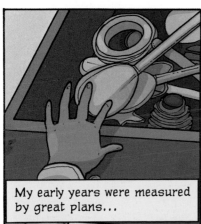

...and unexpected consequences.

5

Skipping ahead to my school years, we'll call this stunt:

THE GREAT SANDWICH CAPER

Now, when I say "unexpected consequences..."

...I'm not suggesting my plans didn't work.

They worked! They did!

But you can't plan for everything.

Right?

6

THE GROCERY JOB

Of course, the key to the success of any plan is to get the right people involved, on both sides.

The takers...

...and the takees.

5¢
DOZEN

BUS...

THE Purloined PIG

Picking the right chump is vital.

THE CANE MUTINY

And we got pretty good at picking chumps out of a crowd.

THE ICE-CREAM CON

More and more, the "we" became me and Prudence, my favorite partner.

I don't know that I ever thought twice about the folks we swindled.

ONE, PLEASE.

WHAT HORROR!

POLICE! HE'S SERVING *PIXIE ICE!*

I'M OUT OF HERE!

I figured, if they were dumb enough to fall for it, then they deserved to lose.

And no harm done. Right?

The Failed Flamingo Filching

Some of our adventures were downright risky...

...but I felt invincible in my poppa's cowhide jacket.

It was the only thing of his we didn't hock after he died of the fever.

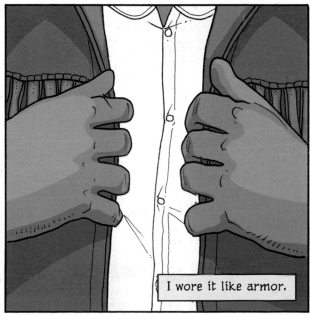

I wore it like armor.

I mostly tried to keep my shenanigans from my momma.

She had enough to worry about.

HEY! YOU DIDN'T PAY FOR LUNCH YET!

FOR THAT HASH? YOU SHOULD BE PAYING ME, COOKIE.

She took care of me, half the neighborhood, and a few stray animals besides.

GET BACK HERE, YOU HOBGOBLIN!

HA!

THIRD FREELOADER THIS WEEK. DON'T KNOW HOW I'M GOING TO AFFORD FIXING THAT OVEN.

But folk disrespecting Momma? Well, that chapped my hide.

So I devised:

The Bowler Hat Heist

This wasn't just about making sport of someone I didn't like or scoring a bit of glory. Now I was feeling the rush of justice.

I felt sure I'd found my calling.

SWIPE

Momma didn't seem pleased to share the spoils.

The Fat Banker Fiasco

But I'd had a taste of justice now, and I began to set my sights higher.

FLIP

WHOOOOOA!

POP

What if I could scheme my way into *real* money, enough so Momma wouldn't have to sell the bakery?

She'd understand then, right? She might even be proud.

But there were always those...

...unexpected consequences.

WHAT HAVE I DONE TO DESERVE YOU? HAVEN'T I RAISED YOU RIGHT?

It was the first time I'd ever seen her cry.

I decided then to quit my scheming and be a good, honest boy...

...after one last caper...

...a big one, something that could end her troubles for good.

I began to plot.

I began to plan.

Prudence was game for whatever I could think up, so long as she got her part of the loot. Never knew a pixie with such an appetite for hats.

One morning as Pru and I brainstormed potential marks, Blunderboar came to Momma's bakery on his weekly visit.

Blunderboar.

13

Giant.

Big business boss.

Filthy rich with his fingers in a lot of political pies.

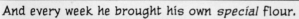
And every week he brought his own *special* flour.

Nutcase.

Something about him gave me the creeps.

C.R.A.C.K

YOU'LL NEED TO PAY FOR THAT.

I COULD SHUT DOWN YOUR PATHETIC BAKERY WITH ONE LETTER TO THE CITY COVEN. JUST KEEP BAKING MY BREAD, AND WE'LL BE PLEASANT NEIGHBORS.

THERE'S NO WAY WE CAN PAY TO HAVE THAT FIXED. WE'RE TWO WEEKS BEHIND IN RENT AS IT IS.

JACK, BE USEFUL FOR ONCE AND TAKE CARE OF IT.

I knew just what to do.

The BLUNDERBOAR BUSINESS

Step 1: Snooping

IF YOU WER... BLUNDERBOAR, WHERE WOULD YOU KEEP YOUR VALUABLES?

UP THERE, TUCKED SAFELY AWAY IN MY NIFTY FLOATING PENTHOUSE.

YEP. THAT'S WHAT I WAS AFRAID OF.

15

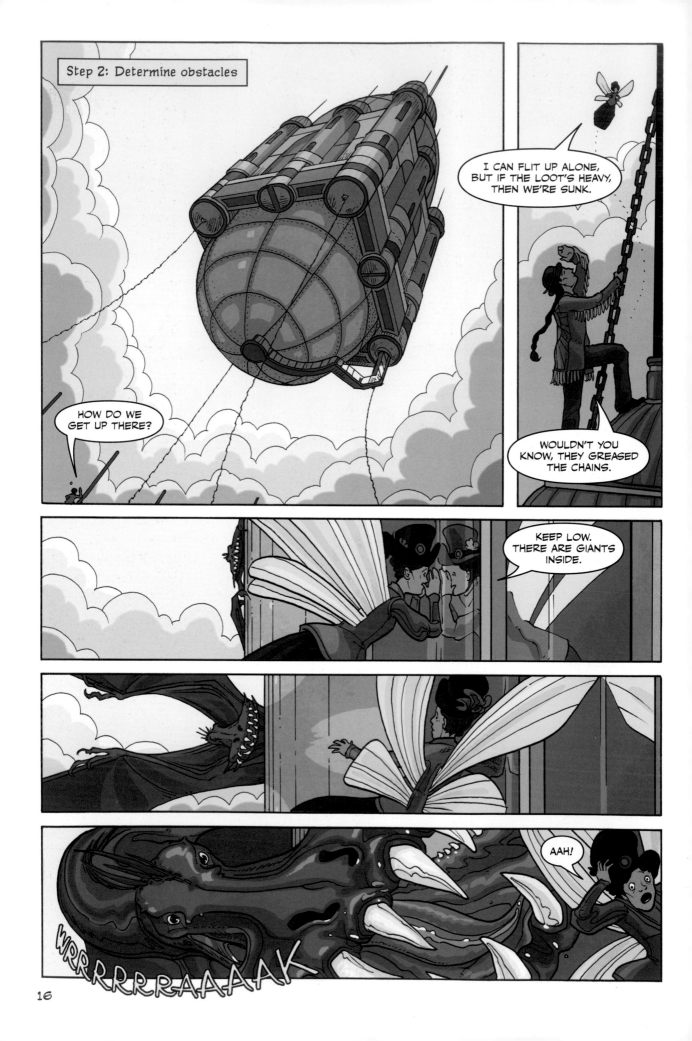

Step 2: Determine obstacles

HOW DO WE GET UP THERE?

I CAN FLIT UP ALONE, BUT IF THE LOOT'S HEAVY, THEN WE'RE SUNK.

WOULDN'T YOU KNOW, THEY GREASED THE CHAINS.

KEEP LOW. THERE ARE GIANTS INSIDE.

AAH!

WRRRRRRAAAAK

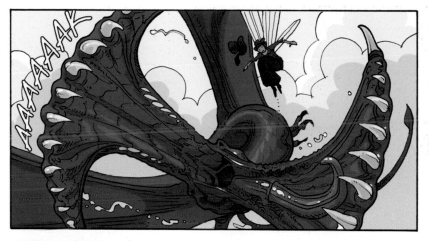

MY HAT!

CHOMP

QUICK, STROLL, STROLL!

WHAT?

STROLL AROUND, PRETEND LIKE YOU CAN'T FLY BEFORE IT EATS YOU!

PRETEND?!

SUCH A LOVELY DAY FOR A STROLL...

...THE JABBERWOCK...

I SEE IT. I SEE IT.

IT'S CIRCLING AGAIN!...

I'M A ROCK... JUST A ROCK, SITTING HERE...

NICE ROCK IMPERSONATION. THE BEAST PASSED US OVER.

COCKY 'WOCKS CAN'T STAND ANYTHING ELSE THAT FLIES.

BUT DID IT *HAVE* TO EAT MY BEST HAT?

YEP. I WAS AFRAID OF SOMETHING LIKE THIS.

Some fancy folk had guard beasts on their roofs to keep birds and nosy flying folk at a distance. None were so deadly as a jabberwock.

17

It could have been Prudence and not just her hat snapped by that creature's jaws. Besides, Blunderboar was not a person to cross lightly. I was thinking of scouting out a new target....

JACK, COME HERE A MINUTE.

TIME YOU HAD THIS.

It was her grandfather's war band. He'd been the chief of his clan and a hero besides. She'd told me stories, but she'd never let me touch it, let alone...

She didn't explain, but I just knew—Momma guessed what I was trying to do and gave me her blessing.

Danger or not, I was determined not to let her down.

Step 3: Make the plan

The jabberwock ate anything that flew but didn't bother giants climbing the ladder they sometimes lowered down. So, if we had our own ladder...

So I...never mind.

We needed funds to buy supplies, and cash was not flowing in those days.

I had to find something to pawn.

YOU ALL RIGHT?

FINE.

I still can't even think about it.

Feeling defenseless without my jacket (not to mention *cold*), I went with Pru in search of something spiffy that'd get us past the jabberwock.

'Course, to score the unusual niceties smuggled in from the Old World, you've got to skulk to a market that's just a touch *black*.

Step 4: Gather equipment

I wanted to go from the ground straight up to the floating penthouse...

...bypass the jabberwock's perch...

...all without flying.

What could we use as an insanely tall ladder?

If those beans grew as fast and tall as promised...

SNAP

SNAP
SNAP
SNAP

SNAP
POP

I NEVER DID TRUST VEGETABLES.

DOGGONE IT, WE'VE BEEN HOODWINKED! NOW WE'LL HAVE TO GET OUR HANDS ON MORE DOUGH TO BUY SOMETHING ELSE.

COO! COO! COO!

Lousy, useless beans! A powerful ache in my gut told me I'd lost my poppa's jacket for nothing.

I kept one, just to remind me not to be stupid and trust magic again.

That night, I returned late from an unsuccessful pursuit of an illicit financial opportunity.

Step 5: See the plan through

WELL, IF THAT DON'T BEAT ALL...

I was afraid Prudence would be sore, but I couldn't spare the time to go find her.

Those giants could have discovered the beanstalk at any moment. I had to act quickly.

I'd climbed past the beast and gained the floating penthouse. Luck was mine.

BLUNDERBOAR, SIR, THE MEN ARE READY TO ATTACH THE OMNIPHONE PIPING IN THE PENTHOUSE.

THIS WRETCHED GOOSE IS BEING UNCOOPERATIVE WITH ITS ALLEGED GOLDEN EGGS.

MAY AS WELL GO HAVE A LOOK.

GOLDEN EGGS, EH? THAT'LL DO.

SQUAWK!

SHH.

...YOU KNOW HOW BLUNDERBOAR IS...

WON'T ALLOW HIS PRECIOUS THINGS TO BE UNGUARDED FOR A MINUTE.

TIFFANY, THAT YOU? YOU SEEN MY SHOWER CAP?

SQUAWK?

WHAT WAS THAT NOISE?

JUST LUMPY, HOLLERING AGAIN.

HEY, YOU TRY SHOWERING WITHOUT GETTING YOUR HAIR WET.

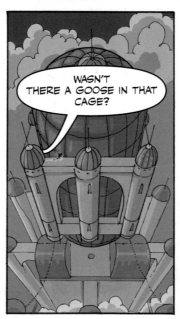

WASN'T THERE A GOOSE IN THAT CAGE?

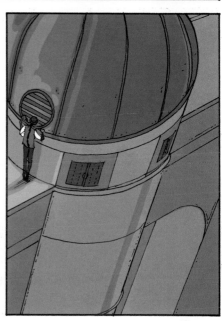

KRAKOWKRAKOWKRAKOWK

KRAKOWKRAKOWKRAKOW

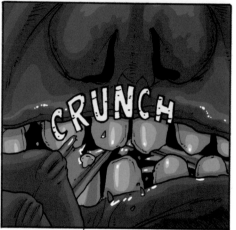

CRUNCH

KRAKOWKRAKOW

IF THAT GOOSE MANAGES TO FLY OFF THE ZEPPELIN AND GETS EATEN BY MR. JABBERS, BLUNDERBOAR WILL SQUEEZE OUR EYEBALLS FOR JUICE.

GOOD POINT. I'LL GO REEL IN THE 'WOCK, JUST IN CASE.

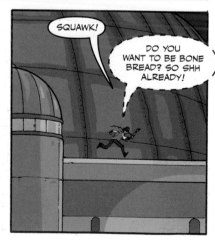

SQUAWK!

DO YOU WANT TO BE BONE BREAD? SO SHH ALREADY!

URK...

CLANG

HHHHU!

KRUMP

...CAN'T FIND THAT GOOSE.

I THOUGHT I HEARD SOMETHING OVER HERE.

HAS THAT BIG PLANT ALWAYS BEEN THERE?

I'M NOT GONNA MAKE IT, I'M NOT GONNA MAKE IT...

MAYBE MR. B IS STARTING A GARDEN. REMINDS ME OF THE GIANT ORCHARDS OF...WAIT, DO YOU SMELL A HUMAN?

OOOF!

WHOA!

SQUAWK!

SQUAWK!

And so I had to hop from rooftop to rooftop, hunting down the goose I'd only just stolen.

All night long.

No rest for the wicked, Momma would say.

SQUAWK!

GOTCHA!

Finally got home near dawn, wondering how I was ever going to sleep again after what I'd seen in Blunderboar's penthouse, when—

CREEEEEEWEAK

WHAT'S GOING ON? IS IT AN EARTHQUAKE?

GREAT JEHOSHAPHAT!

THAT BEANSTALK'S GOING TO TAKE DOWN THE TENEMENT!

SOMETHING'S GROWING OUT THERE!

GET OUT OF THE BUILDING!

WHOK

WHOK

WHOK

IT'S COMING DOWN!

WHOK

DOES MR. B KNOW HIS PLANT IS UPROOTING A BUILDING?

THE BOSS DIDN'T DO THIS.

GET OFF THE BEANSTALK!

DID YOU HEAR ME?

I'VE CHOPPED THROUGH, IT'S GOING TO—

YOU!

UH...

DRIP

DON'T MOVE!

Things looked a mite rickety at the tenement.

THAT'S EVERYONE...

...AND JUST IN—

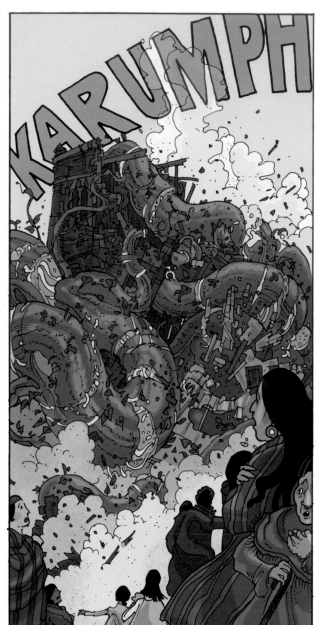

KARUMPH

MOMMA! YOU'RE ALL RIGHT? YOU DIDN'T GET HURT?

THIS WAS YOU, WASN'T IT?

ME? I DIDN'T—

DON'T YOU STAND IN FRONT OF ME WITH OUR HOME AND BAKERY A HEAP OF BRICKS, NOT EVEN THE TINTYPE OF YOUR FATHER SAVED, AND LIE TO ME...

I'M SORRY, MOMMA.

I WAS JUST TRYING TO... I MESSED UP AGAIN, BUT I'LL FIX IT ALL.

I'LL BUILD US A NEW ONE, I'LL—

ENOUGH, JACK.

BUT THIS TIME I REALLY HAVE A WAY TO MAKE LOTS OF GOLD FAST.

I MEAN, YOU TRUST ME, RIGHT? THAT'S WHY YOU GAVE ME THIS...

I THOUGHT IT'D HELP YOU REMEMBER YOUR ROOTS, TO TRY TO BE GOOD FOR ONCE! INSTEAD YOU LIE AND SCHEME AND DESTROY EVERYTHING, EVERYTHING... I CAN'T TALK TO YOU RIGHT NOW.

JUST GO.

JUST GO.

WHERE IS THE DOOMED BOY WHO KILLED ONE OF MY GIANTS?

And so I went.

37

I figured she'd be better off without me, and with Blunderboar's giants on the lookout, there didn't seem to be much good in sticking around.

I hopped the iron horse headed Out West and didn't get off until we stopped somewhere I'd never heard of.

My plan was to hide from the giants, wait for Goldy to lay some eggs, then head back to make things up with Momma—build the nicest tenement and bakery in all the New World Territories. Show her I could be good.

Then things got complicated.

But sometimes that's a good thing.

Long story short...my friend Rapunzel turned around the cesspool that was Gothel's Reach. I guess I helped some, and that last bean did a bit of good.

And now I'm coming home, Momma.

THE REACH

I'm coming home.

I'd hoped three days on the iron horse would give me time to come up with a plan, but we kept busy.

Rapunzel made friends right away. Some of them even had paper money to gamble, but she insisted we just play friendly games.

She would.

I also happened to notice that she looked pretty good by the light of a kerosene lamp.

Whether we were gaming or resting, eating or gabbing, she kept her braids close at hand in case there was trouble.

I almost had her convinced we were leaving the lawless West behind and heading toward safe civilization when...

CHAKA CHAKA

CHAKA CHAKA

IS THE IRON HORSE SUPPOSED TO DO THAT?

ANT PEOPLE CONTINUE ASSAULT ON SHYPORT

YOU MEAN MAKE THAT OMINOUS SOUND AND LURCH UNPLEASANTLY? I SURE HOPE NOT.

43

UUH...

SOME HELP HERE!

44

EEEEEE!

...EEEEEE...

...EEEEEE...

...EEEEEE...

BLAM
BLAM

RIP

TCHUNK

POW

SCREEEEEEEEECH

THANKS FOR BREAKING MY FALL.

UH-HUH. BUT NEXT TIME, *YOU* GET TO BREAK *MY* FALL.

DEAL.

SURE ENOUGH, NOTHIN' BUT NICE, SAFE CIVILIZATION OUT HERE.

YEAH...

When we caught up with the rest of the train, the monsters were gone.

NEVER FEAR, SMALL FOLK!

BLUNDERBOAR AND COMPANY DISCOVERED THE ANT PEOPLE'S NEFARIOUS PLOT TO DESTROY THIS IRON HORSE. WE HAVE CHASED THEM BACK INTO THEIR DANK HOLES.

HOORAY!

PRAISE BE!

I SWEAR, THOSE ANT PEOPLE WOULD'VE BURNED SHYPORT TO THE GROUND LONG AGO IF NOT FOR BLUNDERBOAR.

BLUNDERBOAR? ISN'T THAT THE ONE YOU—

YEAH, THE VERY SAME GIANT. LET'S MAKE OURSELVES SCARCE.

HEY...WEREN'T THERE BOXES IN HERE BEFORE?

MAYBE THEY FELL OUT WHEN THE IRON HORSE DERAILED.

BUT THIS CAR STAYED UPRIGHT.

YOU ARE SAFE NOW!

ALL ABOARD FOR SHYPORT!

WHAT A BUNCH OF MORONS.

HEH. YOU GOT THAT RIGHT.

DID THEY... DID THEY JUST CALL US A BUNCH OF MORONS?

YEAH, I WONDER WHAT THEY MEANT...

BESIDES THAT WE'RE A BUNCH OF MORONS?

CLAKITY-CLAKITY-CLAKITY

RIGHT. BESIDES THAT.

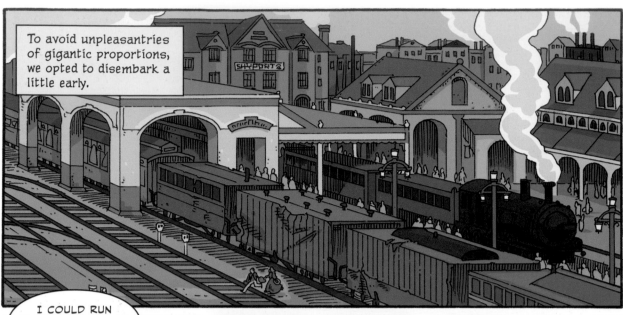

To avoid unpleasantries of gigantic proportions, we opted to disembark a little early.

I COULD RUN FASTER IF I WASN'T WEIGHED DOWN IN THIS GETUP.

IT'S WHAT LADIES WEAR IN THE CITY. YOU DON'T WANT TO LOOK, WELL...

LOOK WHAT?

I DON'T KNOW... UNSOPHISTICATED. BACKWATER.

YOU THINK I'M BACKWATER?

UH-OH, MORE OF 'EM. KEEP MOVING.

WHAT'S THAT NOISE?

IT'S AN OMNIPHONE. RUNS ON STEAM OR SOMETHING, AND MUSIC OR NEWS COMES RIGHT OUT.

YOU'RE PULLING MY LEG NOW.

NO MA'AM, YOU JUST WAIT UNTIL WE GET INTO THE REAL CITY, WONDERS LIKE YOU NEVER IMAGINED.

GOOD EVENING, SHYPORT, AND WELCOME TO THE BLUNDERBOAR HOUR.

HURRY, IT'S ON!

HOW DID THAT OLD COOT GET A WHOLE HOUR ON THE OMNIPHONE?

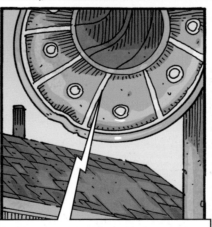

TONIGHT I HOST OPERA SINGER TEMPERANCE GRAVES AND COMEDIAN SNARTY MCFEE. BUT FIRST, AN UPDATE ON THE WAR. MY GIANTS HAVE HAD GREAT SUCCESS IN OGREVILLE AND DUGGERTON...

DID HE SAY WAR?

PROBABLY JUST BEING DRAMATIC. COME ON, I CAN'T WAIT FOR YOU TO SEE THE REAL CITY.

Out West, Rapunzel was a hero, and I was...well, I was sort of her sidekick.

But now we were on my turf, and I couldn't wait for her to see Jack of Shyport in charge, in fashion, in his element.

Then we got to my old neighborhood, Clan Park.

JACK, DID THE BEANSTALK DO ALL THIS DAMAGE?

NO! THIS IS... THIS IS...

I was speechless.

LOOKY HERE.

JACK THE BAKER'S SON

WANTED for KILLING a GIANT

REWARD

BLUNDERBOAR & CO.

WONDERFUL...

MOMMA?

PUNZIE, DISTRACT THOSE GIANTS—WITHOUT WHIPPING THEM, I MEAN.

WHAT? BUT I DON'T—

QUICK, BEFORE THEY GO INSIDE!

56

BUT I...I HAVE GOLD, ENOUGH TO REBUILD THE TENEMENT AND THE BAKERY, AND I THOUGHT—

JUST GO BACK WHEREVER YOU WERE. STAY FAR AWAY.

GET BACK HERE.

WHAT WERE YOU DOING?

THOUGHT I SAW SOMETHING IN THE RUBBLE THAT WAS MINE.

BUT IT WAS NOTHING.

I ACTUALLY THOUGHT SHE MIGHT FORGIVE ME.

COME ON, BEFORE YOU'RE RECOGNIZED.

BLUNDERBOAR

MAYBE IT'S NOT YOU, JACK. SOMETHING'S STRANGE.

WHAT IS SHE DOING WITH BLUNDERBOAR'S GIANTS?

IT'LL BE NIGHT SOON. WE SHOULD FIND A PLACE TO HUNKER DOWN.

57

THIS IS MY AUNT GWEN'S FLAT. IF SHE'S STILL HERE, SHE'LL LEND US A CORNER.

KEEP OUT

AAAH!

SLAM

UH, AUNT GWEN? IT'S ME, JACK. CAN WE COME IN?

...HAVE YOU SEEN THEM, JACKIE? HAVE YOU SEEN THEM?

SEEN WHAT?

WHERE ARE YOU?

THE *ANTS!*

BUGS THAT WALK LIKE MEN! ANT PEOPLE, JACKIE! ANT *PEOPLE!*

WHUH?

YAH!

PEOPLE GO MISSING ALL THE TIME. YOU REMEMBER DOBBIN PUTTERKIN, THE DUGGER WITH THE VEGETABLE STAND ON SLIM STREET?

YEAH...

HE WAS EATEN! AND OFFICER GURNEY?

SO—

EATEN! AND CRAZY OLD PHILOMENA ZEP?

EATEN!!

LISTEN, I JUST SAW MY MOTHER AND I'VE GOT TO—

PSSHT! YOU'VE GOT TO STOP CAUSING TROUBLE FOR HER. BLUNDERBOAR'S LOCKED HER UP TO BAKE HIS BREAD AND NEVER LETS HER OUT WITHOUT A GUARD.

HE'S...HE'S HOLDING HER? THAT SWINDLING, DEEPLY ROTTEN—

SAYS SHE AIN'T GOIN' NOWHERE TILL HE GETS HIS HANDS ON HER MURDEROUS SON.

IF I TURN MYSELF OVER TO HIM, HE'LL LET HER GO?

YOU'RE BAD NEWS, SONNY. NOW OUT BEFORE SOMEONE SEES YOU AND LOCKS ME UP TOO! SHOO!

SLAM

SO...THAT WAS YOUR AUNT, HUH? I COULD SEE THE FAMILY RESEMBLANCE IN HER, UH, NOSE.

YEAH...

HE'S HOLDING HER IN THAT FORTRESS OF A...

PROPERTY FOR LEASE SPACIOUS ROOMS NICE VIEW

C'MON, I'VE GOTTA SEE SOMETHING.

I'D WAGER MY GOOSE...

...THAT BLUNDERBOAR'S MADE SOME IMPROVEMENTS IN SECURITY...

...SINCE I WALTZED IN ON A BEANSTALK.

LET'S JUST SEE...

...WHAT THEY MIGHT BE.

CLACK

NOTHING'S OUT THERE.

I'M REELING THE BROWNIES BACK IN.

HIC

ERK

eeeeee

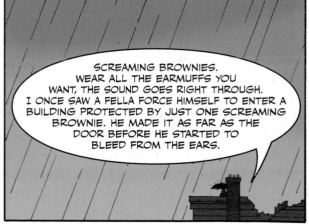

SCREAMING BROWNIES. WEAR ALL THE EARMUFFS YOU WANT, THE SOUND GOES RIGHT THROUGH. I ONCE SAW A FELLA FORCE HIMSELF TO ENTER A BUILDING PROTECTED BY JUST ONE SCREAMING BROWNIE. HE MADE IT AS FAR AS THE DOOR BEFORE HE STARTED TO BLEED FROM THE EARS.

AND BLUNDERBOAR HAS DOZENS OF THEM CHAINED IN THOSE CELLS.

CHAINED... THAT'S HORRIBLE! WE'VE GOT TO—

WHAT, BLEED FROM OUR EARS? COOL YOUR HEELS, THEY'RE PROBABLY PAID EMPLOYEES.

PAID TO BE CHAINED UP?

EH, BROWNIES ARE WEIRD THAT WAY. ANYWAY, FIRST PRIORITY IS MY MOTHER. WE CAN LIBERATE THE ALARM SYSTEM LATER.

HMM.

YAH!

WHAT? OH! EW. UM...JACK, CAN THOSE THINGS SEE US?

PROBABLY THE JABBERWOCK CAN.

THE...UH... BANDERSNATCH, I DON'T KNOW. IN ANY CASE, IT MIGHT BE A GOOD IDEA TO GET OUT OF SPITTING RANGE.

BANDERSNATCHES SPIT?

WITHOUT GETTING INTO TOO MUCH FLESH-BURNING DETAIL, YEAH, PUNZIE, THEY SPIT.

JACK, THIS PLACE IS INSANE.

YEP. HOME.

EVERYTHING'S JUST DAISY, ISN'T IT?

IT'S NO BOWL OF CHICKEN SOUP, THAT'S FOR SURE. LET'S GET A WIGGLE ON.

MY MOMMA LOOKED SO SAD... SHE'S NOT LIKE THAT. SHE'S FEISTY.

WE'LL GET HER OUT. PICK UP THE PACE THERE.

RAPUNZEL, THERE'S NOWHERE TO GO.

DON'T YOU HAVE ANY FRIENDS?

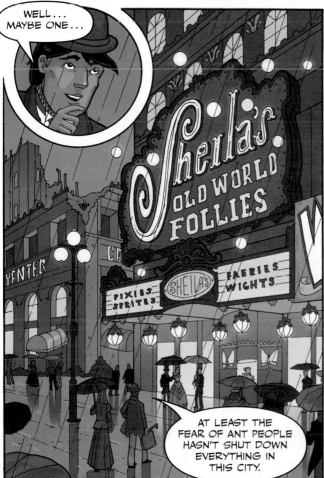

WELL... MAYBE ONE...

AT LEAST THE FEAR OF ANT PEOPLE HASN'T SHUT DOWN EVERYTHING IN THIS CITY.

Sheila's OLD WORLD FOLLIES

PIXIES SPRITES SHEILA'S FAERIES WIGHTS

YENTER

STAGE DOOR

THE GAL IN PURPLE ON THE END? THAT'S PRUDENCE. WE USED TO RUN TOGETHER.

RUN?

UH...WORK TOGETHER.

BUT WHAT... WHAT ARE THEY?

63

PIXIES.

NOW THERE'S THE WIDE-EYED LOOK OF A...

IF YOU SAY "BACKWATER GIRL," I'M GOING TO KICK YOU IN THE SHINS.

BUT WOW. THAT'S...WOW.

SEE? I TOLD YOU THERE WERE WONDERS.

HIYA PRU, YOU'RE LOOKIN' SWELL. THIS IS MY FRIEND RAPUNZEL.

JACKIE! LONG TIME NO SEE, CHIEF.

WELCOME, HONEY. ANY FRIEND OF JACKIE'S MUST BE A-OK.

HOW'S SCHEMES?

SINCE YOU GHOSTED OFF, MY SALARY HERE HAS BEEN PAYING THE RENT, BUT IT'S NOT NEARLY ENOUGH TO KEEP ME IN HATS.

A MILLION GOLD COINS WOULDN'T BE ENOUGH TO KEEP YOU IN HATS.

HYSTERICAL.

ANYWAY, I'M READY TO GET BACK INTO THE GAME. WHAT'S THE NEW HEIST?

HEIST?

WHAT A SILLY—WHY WOULD I—AHEM, PUNZIE AND I ARE TRYING TO LAY LOW. CAN WE SLEEP AT YOUR PLACE TONIGHT?

SURE THING, JACKIE, BUT AREN'T YOU DYING TO CRACK OPEN BLUNDERBOAR'S GIANT FLOATING TREASURE HOUSE AND SEE WHAT'S INSIDE?

"CRACK OPEN BLUNDERBOAR'S..." HA! YOU ALWAYS WERE A CRACK-UP, PRU.

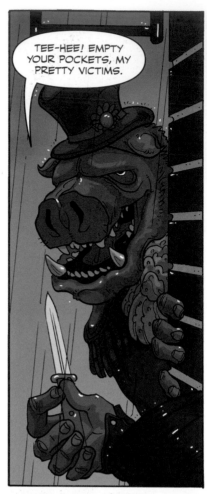

TEE-HEE! EMPTY YOUR POCKETS, MY PRETTY VICTIMS.

WHUP

FWIT

CH-KRAK

GET LOST, NUMBSKULL.

YOU SURE KNOW YOUR WAY AROUND THE STREETS, HONEY.

Isn't she fantastic? I thought about telling her so right then and there, but Rapunzel's not the type of girl who cares about sappy compliments.

NOT REALLY. I'M FROM OUT WEST, BUT BAD GUYS ARE THE SAME NO MATTER WHERE YOU ARE.

I was hoping Prudence would keep her lips buttoned about how I'd been one of those bad guys.

Rapunzel knew I had a sordid past...

...but I'd never offered details on the whole preying-on-the-innocent-for-profit parts. I reckoned if she knew, she'd split and never look back.

We got to Pru's...

...took the visitor's entrance...

...and curled up for the night.

The next morning, Prudence spilled the beans on Shyport's crazy year.

Shyport extra!

MAYOR RENEWS BLUNDERBOAR·CO'S CONTROL OF SECURITY

ANTS BURN FACTORY

SMOKE RISES OVER

TWELVE MISSING FROM DUGGERTON

CITIZENS OF SHYPORT'S

ARE SQUIRREL EVIL?

Apparently the city had been falling apart until Blunderboar stepped in.

SO HE'S CONTROLLING THE POLICE FORCE?

HE *IS* THE POLICE FORCE.

THIS IS DEPRESSING. I NEED A CUPCAKE.

MAYBE I'D BETTER TURN MYSELF OVER TO HIM.

DON'T YOU DARE! DIDN'T YOU TELL ME HE GRINDS HUMAN BONES INTO FLOUR?

THAT'S SURE WHAT IT LOOKED LIKE...

HEY, YOU KNOW, I SAW SOME HUGE THINGS WITH CLAWS UP THERE, TOO, UNLESS I DREAMED IT. MAYBE THEY WERE THESE SAME ANT PEOPLE.

THAT WAS LONG BEFORE THEY SUPPOSEDLY DUG THEIR WAY UP TO SHYPORT.

THE BARKING DRYAD

BLUNDERBOAR, YOU DEMON, WHAT ARE YOU UP TO?

SPARKSMITH... THAT WAS THE LABEL ON THOSE CRATES FROM THE IRON HORSE...

...THE ONES THAT WENT MISSING—

CONVENIENTLY RIGHT AFTER THE ANT PEOPLE ATTACKED.

HEY, PRU, KNOW WHERE WE CAN FIND THE *SHYPORT SHEET* OFFICE?

MY HAT!

After a brief detour to Pru's for another hat, we made our stealthy way to Turich Street.

WHAT—*ACK!*

WHAT'S THAT NOISE? IS IT ANOTHER SHYPORT WONDER?

ODORLESS EXCAVATOR

LATRINES EMPTIED

THRUM-THRUM-THRUM-THRUM-THRUM

I'M NOT SURE...

70

I TELL YOU, I WILL NOT BE BULLIED, YOU BULLYING BULLIES, YOU!

I WILL NOT—

I SAY, I WON'T—

I'M NOT MOVING! I WILL PROTECT THIS NEWSPAPER WITH MY LAST BREATH.

HE'S GOING TO GET HIMSELF KILLED!

WHAT A NUTJOB.

UM.

COME ON, WE'VE GOT TO SAVE HIM.

C'MON!

RIGHT. OKAY. SAVE HIM.

73

MOVE!

JACK!!

OOF!

KRUSH

AAH, IT'S BREAKING...GET READY...IT'S YOUR TURN...

MY TURN FOR WHAT?

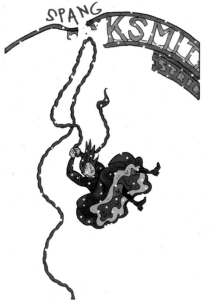

SPANG

AAK!

WHUMP

OW.

TO BREAK MY FALL. WHAT A GENTLEMAN.

MY PLEASURE.

UH-OH.

...MAY TAKE DOWN ONE BUILDING...NEVER STOP THE SPARKSMITHS, MY FRIENDS...

HE SOUNDS FUNNY. I THINK HE GOT HIS HEAD CLUNKED.

OR ELSE HE'S JUST A FANATIC ADMIRER OF PUDDING.

PISTACHIO PUDDING IS AWFULLY TASTY...

WHO ISN'T?

Did I just see what I thought I saw?

So we introduced ourselves to Frederick Sparksmith the Third and chatted about this and that—you know, the weather, the best sausage vendors, how behemoth insects had conveniently destroyed businesses that competed with Blunderboar's empire.

The boxes on the train? The young Sparksmith had ordered materials for building Ant People traps in an attempt to protect his businesses.

Unfortunately, all his cargo mysteriously went missing from the iron horse.

BLUNDERBOAR CHOOSES TO FIGHT THE ANT PEOPLE WHEREVER HE'D LIKE SOME DAMAGE DONE, THAT'S WHAT I SAY.

ACTUALLY, I THINK BLUNDERBOAR AND THE ANT PEOPLE ARE... ARE *ALLIES* OR SOMETHING, WORKING TOGETHER TO DESTROY COMPETITION UNDER THE GUISE OF URBAN WARFARE.

ANYTHING?

NOT THAT I COULD SEE.

BLUNDERBOAR MUST HAVE PEOPLE IN THE TRADE COMMISSION AND HAVE KNOWN ABOUT YOUR SHIPMENT. THE ANT PEOPLE PROBABLY ATTACKED THE IRON HORSE JUST TO STEAL YOUR SUPPLIES.

THOSE RAPSCALLIONS! THOSE VAGABONDS! WELL, THEIR GAME IS UP. I SHALL SIMPLY LOOK THOSE GIANTS IN THE EYE—

THEN YOU'D BETTER STAND ON A STOOL.

...AHEM, AND DEMAND, OH UNSCRUPULOUS GIANTS, LET THIS CITY GO! YOU CLAIM ANT PEOPLE ARE THE REAL THREAT?

BALDERDASH!

YEAH, THAT'S A REAL SLICK PLAN FOR A FIRST TRY, BUT THERE MIGHT BE A HITCH OR TWO ON IMPLEMENTATION. IF—

SKREEEE

LOOK OUT!

WHISH

YEE-HA!

SSSSSSSS

LET'S HIGHTAIL IT, FOLKS. THOSE PEBBLES WON'T HOLD IT FOR LONG.

TING

TING

KRUMP

I SAY...AHEM...I, UH...HELLO, RAPUNZEL, WAS IT? I'M FREDDIE, AND YOU'RE...YOU'RE TALENTED, I SAY, AND QUITE THE CREATURE.

UH, THANKS, UM, YOU'RE A NICE... CREATURE, TOO.

ANT PEOPLE *AND* GIANTS? THAT'LL BE ONE TOUGH TREASURE HOUSE TO LIBERATE.

Did he touch her hand?

NONSENSE! THROUGH THE DUST OF VALOROUS ACTION, YOUR ENCHANTING EYES GLEAM ALL THE BRIGHTER.

LOOK, I DON'T THINK IT'LL BE SAFE FOR YOU TO GO HOME, FREDDIE. BLUNDERBOAR MIGHT SEND ANT PEOPLE TO FINISH THE JOB. YOU HAVE A PLACE YOU CAN HIDE OUT?

INDEED. UH...

MY LADY, COULD I...WOULD YOU AND YOUR FRIENDS CARE TO ACCOMPANY ME TO... MY WORKSHOP IS A LITTLE RUSTIC...

BUT I COULD OFFER YOU SOME REFRESHMENT.

OR PING-PONG?

IT'S THE LATEST NOVELTY. WHEN THE BALLS BOUNCE, THEY MAKE THE MOST ENCHANTING POPPING SOUNDS.

MM-MM. NOTHING A PIXIE NEEDS LIKE A LITTLE REFRESHMENT, AND/OR PING-PONG.

I WOULDN'T MIND A CHANGE OF GARB AND A WASHUP. I FEEL HALF-BURIED AND MY HAIR'S FIT FOR A VERMIN'S NEST.

GOLLY, THANKS, FREDDIE.

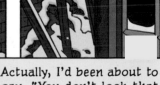

I'd had those very words on the tip of my tongue but loudmouth blurted first.

Actually, I'd been about to say, "You don't look that bad," which is basically the same thing.

79

Instead we trudged over to his workshop near Duggerton, and all the while I was trying to figure what to do.

Too bad we couldn't risk stopping at the Sparksmith mansion in Marble Heights. Freddie probably had gold-plated toilet bowls he was dying to flaunt for Rapunzel.

I could work up a plan to get Momma free from her guards the next time she left the building...

...but that wouldn't be good enough. I'd promised her I'd rebuild the tenement and bakery. Can't do that in a war zone.

Besides, Momma's grandpoppa, the great chief, wouldn't run off, knowing what we know about Blunderboar. Wouldn't just stand by while people were suffering.

SO DO YOU SELL THESE, UM, DOOHICKEYS?

NO, NO, COLLECTING GADGETS IS A HOBBY.

NEWSPAPERS, PUBLISHING, THAT'S THE SPARKSMITH LEGACY. GRANDPOP ALWAYS SAID, "A WELL-INFORMED SOCIETY IS THE PINNACLE OF CIVILIZATION."

I'VE RECENTLY...OOF... MADE A MOST INGENIOUS PURCHASE...OUCH...FROM AN OVERSEAS CATALOG...

...THAT WILL SOLVE ALL OUR PROBLEMS!

BEHOLD THE BACKPACK-APULT.

STRAP IN, JACK, I SHALL SIMPLY FLING YOU AT YOUR LOFTY DESTINATION!

It was then I first suspected that Freddie wanted me dead.

UH, NO YOU WON'T. ANYTHING THAT GOES FLYING AT THAT THING RISKS BEING CAUGHT MIDAIR AND GNAWED TO A PULP BY A SKY-JEALOUS JABBERWOCK.

OR FALL SCREAMING TO HIS DEATH ON THE PAVEMENT BELOW...

BUT NICE THINKING, FREDDIE. WE'LL CALL THAT PLAN B.

ANYHOO, WE'VE GOT TO PUBLICLY EXPOSE BLUNDERBOAR'S CONNECTION TO THE ANT PEOPLE.

I HAPPEN TO KNOW A MEDIA MAN WITH HIS OWN NEWSPAPER.

BINGO! FRONT PAGE, SPECIAL EDITION!

WEREN'T YOUR PRINTING PRESSES IN THAT BUILDING THAT JUST COLLAPSED?

RIGHT! ER...

RIGHT. I'LL NEED A NEW PRESS, WON'T I?

IT WON'T BE ENOUGH. THIS CITY'S IN LOVE WITH BLUNDERBOAR. WE NEED DEFINITE PROOF.

LIKE, SAY, AN ANT PERSON WILLING TO SPILL THE BEANS?

THAT'D DO.

Freddie assured us he had enough materials on hand to make one Ant Person trap.

While I helped him put it together, Pru headed out for her evening show. Apparently Rapunzel made an escape, too.

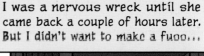

I was a nervous wreck until she came back a couple of hours later. But I didn't want to make a fuss...

83

...so I played it cool.

YOU JUST WENT OUT IN THE CITY? ALONE? BUT WHY? THIS ISN'T OUT WEST, PUNZIE. THE CITY IS DANGEROUS EVEN IF IT WEREN'T CURRENTLY A WAR ZONE.

YOU COULD'VE GOTTEN LOST OR KILLED OR BAKED INTO MUFFINS! WHAT WERE YOU DOING?

NOTHING, FORGET ABOUT IT.

Completely cool.

The next afternoon, we had something that might possibly hold an Ant Person for a minute. If we could find one and ask it nicely to step inside.

Brilliant plan, Jack.

I'LL NEED A FEW HOURS TO DO SOME RESEARCH.

RIGHT-O, CAPTAIN. WE'LL KEEP OURSELVES BUSY WHILE YOU DO THE BRAIN WORK.

MISS RAPUNZEL?

I...UH, I TOOK THE LIBERTY TO ORDER A CAKE. FOR YOU. BECAUSE YOU'RE, YOU KNOW, SWEET. LIKE CAKE. THAT IS, IF YOU'D LIKE SOME. CAKE.

REALLY?

JACK, DO YOU THINK I'M SWEET LIKE CAKE?

NOT ON YOUR LIFE.

OH.

'Cause she's not some silly pastry girl. She's strong and great and amazing and fun and beautiful and—

I LOVE CAKE!

BINGO!

I'D LIKE TO BINGO HIS—

JACKIE, JACKIE...ARE YOU TRYING TO LOSE HER?

WHAT? NO, I—

EE-GADS, BUCKO, GIVE THAT GIRL A FLOWER OR YOU MIGHT BE SAYING TOODLES FOR GOOD.

COME ON, RAPUNZEL DOESN'T WANT A FLOWER.

IN ALL MY DIMINUTIVE YEARS, I'VE NEVER SEEN A GIRL WHO DIDN'T MELT AT GETTING A BLOOM FROM HER FELLA.

85

Pru didn't get it. Rapunzel isn't girly—she's all about action, and the best way to woo her was to show her I was good for something.

Unfortunately, the only thing I've ever been good at is hatching schemes.

The best schemes are a fine balance of the takers and the takees—you've got to have the right people on both sides.

Blunderboar was the kind of mark you find once in a lifetime—wealthy, evil, and due a long crawl in a deep latrine.

But he had a fist the size of a boulder. If I tried to bring him down and failed, I was pretty sure there wouldn't be enough of me left to crawl anywhere.

But my mother had no one else. And Rapunzel expected me to succeed. It would be my greatest scheme ever or a fatal failure.

I perused Freddie's stash of newspapers from the past year...

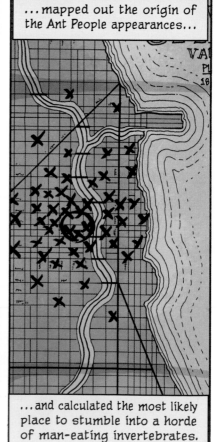

...mapped out the origin of the Ant People appearances...

...and calculated the most likely place to stumble into a horde of man-eating invertebrates.

The darkest, seediest, most unsavory quarter of Shyport...

Troll's Cranny.

If our luck held, we'd have the trap built before anyone tried to knife us.

But as is the case with my luck, it didn't hold.

TONG TONG

OI! DIS 'ERE'S DA COMMODORE'S TURF YE WEE WADDLEPUPPIES.

I looked at that crook and wondered if that's how Rapunzel would see me, once she realized just what I am.

VDAK NK

BAD GUYS SURE ARE BAD, AREN'T THEY?

BAD IS BAD, THAT'S DARN TOOTIN'.

DID HE SAY "WADDLEPUPPY"?

CRUNCH

YOU'LL BE NEEDIN' TO PAY THE STRUTTIN' TOLL, SWEETAH CHEEKUMS.

:CHUNK

I MEAN, IT'S EASY TO TELL WHO THE BAD GUYS ARE.

SURE, THE ONES TRYING TO KILL US.

I was waiting for someone still bigger to show up and take care of this group for us...

...SWEETAH WHAT? WAS THAT AN INSULT?

NOT GETTING PAST US, YOU SPARE-RIBBED CONEY-HACKETS.

...but no such luck.

CONEY-HACKETS? SERIOUSLY. YOU'RE GOING WITH CONEY-HACKETS? YOU GUYS ARE RIDICULOUS.

I wasn't sure Rapunzel would understand how in the city everything is a whole lot trickier.

What would she do if she found out I used to be one of the bad guys?

What if I still am?

HA-HA! I GUESS THOSE VILLAINS DIDN'T LIKE THE LOOK OF US.

OR THEY SAW SOMETHING WORSE...

THIS IS THE PART WHERE WE FLEE FOR OUR LIVES.

RIGHT.

PRU, LET'S DO THE PIXIE SPLIT.

WHAT'S THE MATTER? AFRAID I'LL BITE OFF YOUR NOSE?

A follies gal at heart, Pru could do some fancy flying.

PUNZ, FRED, GET READY TO JUMP LEFT.

THESE FELLERS HERE SAID ANT PEOPLE WERE A BUNCH OF LILY-LIVERED...UM... BUM-SKEETERS!

UH-OH.

WHAM

SKReeeee

FLAP   FLAP   FLAP FLAP

THERE SHE IS. FREDDIE, PUNZIE, CIRCLE BACK.

AYE, CAPTAIN!

FLAP   FLAP FLAP

TALK, YOU!

WHAT...ER... WHAT EXACTLY ARE WE TRYING TO FIND OUT?

RIGHT...

WE'RE GOING TO NEED TO KNOW WHAT THE LARGER PLAN IS...

WHAT'S YOUR PLAN, FIEND?

TELL US!

FLIP FLIP FLIP

...WHAT IS IT THAT BLUNDERBOAR IS ORCHESTRATING THAT REQUIRES ANT PEOPLE?

SKReee

WHAT IS BLUNDERBOAR UP TO, DEMONSPAWN?

WHY WOULD ANT PEOPLE EVEN WORK WITH A GIANT?

WHAT IS HE OFFERING THEM?

WHAT IS HE PAYING YOU!?

We needed to talk to whoever was leading the ants. And get them to turn on Blunderboar.

WHERE IS YOUR LEADER?

SKREE.

WHAT?

SKREE.

ALL WE SEEM TO BE GETTING IS A LOT OF *SKREE.*

I WAS NOTICING THAT MYSELF.

IT DOESN'T MAKE ANY SENSE. THEY HAVE TO BE ABLE TO COMMUNICATE, OR NONE OF THIS WOULD GET ORGANIZED!

TAKE A LOOK AT THIS, CAPTAIN.

JUST JACK IS FINE. WHAT IS IT?

A CLUE... SHROUDED IN MYSTERY BY ARCANE ORIENTISH PAPER-CREASING!

JUST UNFOLD IT, FREDDIE.

OH.

IT GOES WITHOUT SAYING THAT I'LL BE GOING WITH YOU.

LOOK, THIS IS GOING TO REQUIRE SOME SERIOUS FAST-TALKING, AND YOU'LL—

TELL ME YOU'RE NOT WORRIED ABOUT MY SAFETY. YOU DO REMEMBER THE GIANT SNAKE?

IT'S JUST, I'M HOPING TO DO THIS WITHOUT A FIGHT, AND MY... TRICK WILL BE MORE BELIEVABLE IF I'M ALONE.

HMPH.

RIGHT. HMPH.

OKAY. I'LL NEED A...A REAR GUARD.

THAT WAY YOU'LL BE READY TO COME RUNNING IF I NEED HELP.

BUT DON'T COME UNLESS I HOLLER. NO NEED FOR ALL OF US TO LOSE OUR LIVERS.

FINE.

BUT YOU BETTER BE CAREFUL, JACK THE BAKER'S SON.

DON'T WORRY ABOUT ME.

I'M WILY.

Also, fairly stupid.

But only on occasion.

Such as when I'm descending alone into a sewer hive of gargantuan flesh-eating insect people.

But it was the kind of deed that'd make my momma proud, wasn't it?

Right about when that dank, rotten stench hit me I questioned the whole going-it-alone thing.

The sort of thing good guys did?

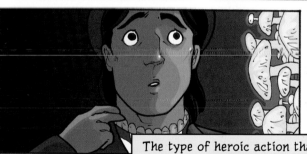

The type of heroic action that Rapunzel could admire.

HELLO?

UM...

ANT PEOPLE?

SKREE?

I'M UNARMED. I'M A...FRIEND. NO NEED FOR BITING OR TEARING OR EATING...

JUST CAME TO TALK.

BLUNDERBOAR SENT ME.

SKREE?

AAH!

OH...GOOD. HERE YOU ARE. JUST AS I...JUST AS BLUNDERBOAR SAID. LISTEN, THERE'S BEEN A CHANGE OF PLANS.

WHAT?

RIGHT. YOU DO SPEAK—*AHEM*. SO, THIS EVENING AT EXACTLY FIVE, BLUNDERBOAR WANTS YOU TO POP UP ON FLEET STREET IN FRONT OF THE *SHYPORT LEDGER* BUILDING, SHOUT *"SKREE"* A LOT, THE USUAL. EXCEPT NO KILLING THIS TIME. WHAT A DRAG, HUH?

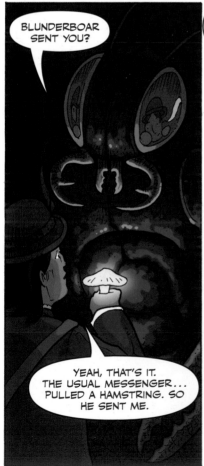

BLUNDERBOAR SENT YOU?

YEAH, THAT'S IT. THE USUAL MESSENGER... PULLED A HAMSTRING. SO HE SENT ME.

HMPH, THERE GOES TONIGHT'S SHUFFLEBONE TOURNAMENT.

DID OUR GALLANT LEADER GIVE A REASON FOR THIS MISSION?

YEAH, I TOLD HIM...

...YOU GUYS WOULDN'T LIKE IT.

BUT YOU KNOW HOW THOSE GIANTS ARE...

...ABOUT KEEPING UP...

...APPEARANCES.

99

WHAT ARE YOU DOING DOWN HERE?

YOU SAID TO COME IF YOU HOLLERED.

WHOOPS. I DID HOLLER, DIDN'T I...

JUST A BIT. SO WHAT'S THE PLAN?

THE PLAN? UH, RUN.

RUN?

RUN!

SPLASH

YOUR PLANS SEEM TO FAVOR THE FLEEING OPTION OF LATE.

I SHOULD'VE GUESSED! I MEAN, WHAT ARE THE ODDS THAT GIANTS AND SOME HITHERTO UNKNOWN BREED OF HUGE INSECT WOULD BE THE SAME SIZE?

WAIT, GIVE ME A MINUTE TO FIGURE IT OUT... CARRY THE TWO...

THE ODDS ARE ZILCH, 'CAUSE THERE'S NO SUCH THING AS ANT PEOPLE.

COO COO

WHAT WAS THAT?

WHAT?

Sorry, Momma. I didn't want you to be right about me, but you were. Sorry.

THAT IMPOSSIBLY LOUD, DEAFENING COO.

OH THAT. I THOUGHT YOU MEANT SOMETHING ELSE.

WHAT THE...

THEY HAVE MAGICKED BIRD BEASTIES!

AAH!

HELP!

Three giant pigeons living in the sewer.

ATTACK! ATTACK!

Three magic beans I tossed at some birds near a sewer grate last year.

Being just a tad distracted, I didn't put the two together at the time.

CHANGE THAT ORDER TO FLEE!

WHAT IS THIS TUNNEL? IT LOOKS FRESHLY DUG.

LESS CONTEMPLATION, MORE FLEEING FOR LIFE.

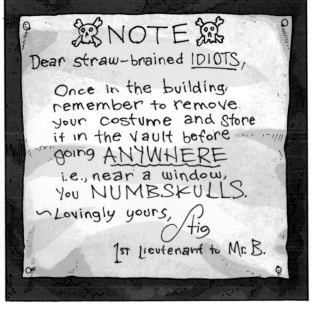

☠ NOTE ☠

Dear straw-brained IDIOTS,

Once in the building, remember to remove your costume and store it in the vault before going ANYWHERE i.e., near a window, you NUMBSKULLS.

Lovingly yours, Stig

1st Lieutenant to Mr. B.

UP THERE'S THE BLUNDERBOAR BUILDING. THEY'VE GOT AN UNDERGROUND ENTRANCE, SO THE ANT PEOPLE CAN SNEAK IN AND OUT WITHOUT BEING SEEN.

THIS IS IT, OUR WAY IN. THEY THINK THEIR FORTRESS IS IMPENETRABLE, SO THEY MIGHT HAVE THEIR GUARD DOWN ON THE INSIDE. BUT IT'S NOW OR NEVER, BEFORE ANY OF THOSE BIRD-HARASSED LUMPS GETS BACK TO REPORT.

YOU AIM TO FREE YOUR MOTHER AND STEAL SOME EVIDENCE OF BLUNDERBOAR'S DECEPTION?

WHAT ABOUT OUR TRAPPED ANT PERSON?

TROLL'S CRANNY IS TEEMING WITH ANT PEOPLE. OURS IS SURELY FREED BY NOW. SO...WE'LL HAVE TO GO THROUGH THE BUILDING UP TO THE ROOF, AND THEN CLIMB INTO THAT FLOATING STORY.

THERE MIGHT STILL BE ANT PEOPLE COSTUMES IN A CLOSET NEAR BLUNDERBOAR'S STATEROOM. THAT MIGHT JUST CONVINCE THE MAYOR AND ALL OF SHYPORT.

HOW DO YOU KNOW WHERE THE COSTUMES WOULD BE?

I'M PRETTY SURE I SAW SOME THE TIME I CLIMBED THE BEANSTALK.

YOU MEAN, YOU'VE ACTUALLY BEEN INSIDE THAT PLACE?

YEAH, JUST FOR A MINUTE.

Most terrifying minute of my short life.

BUT I THOUGHT THE BEANSTALK FELL DOWN AND...AND I DIDN'T KNOW YOU ACTUALLY GOT UP THERE. WHY DIDN'T YOU TELL ME?

'CAUSE I HAD TO SKIP TOWN FAST. AND WE BETTER SKIP THIS SEWER BEFORE WE'RE FOUND.

I sent Prudence off to find my mother in Blunderboar's kitchen, warn her what we were up to...

...and get Momma out of the building if she could, or at least find a good hiding place, in case we got caught.

ROLF, WHERE DID YOU PUT THE BUBBLE BATH?

HEY, WHO—

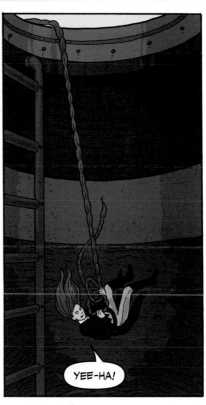

YEE-HA!

UH!

SLIP

SMACK

LET OFF, YOU GNATS!

OW!

UGH.

OOF!

THAT WAS . . .

TOUGH.

YEAH.

FREDDIE, YOU HAVE ANY MORE OF THAT ANT-TRAP WIRE?

WHAM

WHAT? OH? YES, RIGHT-O!

GROOOOAAAN

107

PUNZIE?

YEAH?

YOU— YOU'RE GOOD AT LASSOING STUFF.

THANKS...

Do I tell her she's pretty, that my heart goes *bang* every time she hog-ties a giant, that I have to look away for fear of drowning in her eyes? That I don't want to be a criminal mastermind anymore?

Ah, the words that flow from my mouth are pure poetry....

WHEN WE REACH THE TOP FLOOR, FIND STAIRS TO THE ROOF AND WE'RE NEARLY HOME FREE.

DING

FEE. FI. FO, AND, OH LET'S SAY, *FUM.*

AND YOU SAY, PRUDENCE DEAR, THAT THIS ISN'T THE FIRST TIME HE'S LEFT YOU BEHIND AS HE BREAKS INTO MY HOME? BAD FORM.

HIYA, JACKIE.

Ain't that just daisy.

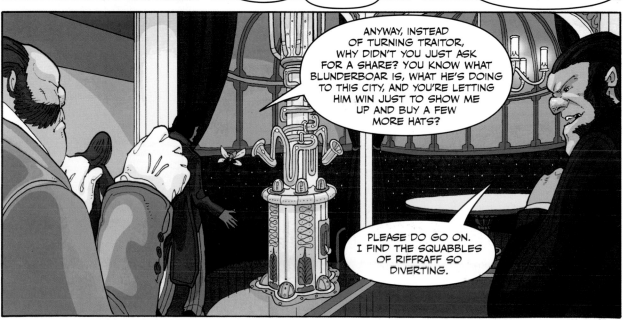

MAUDE, THIS PIXIE HAS PAINTED A VERY INTERESTING STORY OF A BOY WHO PLANS BIG SCHEMES TO GET GAIN, NO MATTER WHOM HE HURTS. WHAT A TRIAL HE MUST HAVE BEEN. MY OWN DEAR MOTHER OFTEN DEPLORED HAVING TO RAISE A SCHEMING GENIUS SON.

I'M NOT LIKE YOU.

YOU BREAK INTO MY HOME...

...STEAL MY GOOSE...

...AND IN THE PROCESS DESTROY A BUILDING AND COMMIT NEGLIGENT GIGANTICIDE.

CLUMSY? YES. PATHETIC? OBVIOUSLY.

BUT GIVE YOU SOME MUSCLE TO BACK YOU UP, REFINE YOUR SENSE OF STYLE AND SHOWMANSHIP...

...AND MY BOY, YOU ARE ME.

IMITATION IS PURE FLATTERY, BUT YOU MAY HAVE GUESSED, I'M NOT FOND OF COMPETITION.

UH, MR. B? I KNOW I SUGGESTED RIPPING SOME LIMBS FROM VARIOUS LIMBS, BUT NOW I'M THINKING, HOW'S ABOUT A GOOD SCOLDING AND SENDING HIM ON HIS WAY?

SHE'S SERVED HER PURPOSE. SOMEBODY STUFF HER IN A BOX.

WHAT?!

HOW DARE YOU, YOU WALKING MUDSLIDE?

JACK, WHAT'S THE PLAN?

PLAN? NO PLAN. IT'S DEAD. I FAILED. THE END.

GET HER!

COME ON, YOU ALWAYS HAVE A PLAN B—

AND THAT PLAN WILL BLOW UP, TOO. I ALWAYS FAIL. RAPUNZEL, IT'S TIME YOU KNEW—I'VE BEEN PRETENDING TO BE THE KIND OF FELLA YOU MIGHT LIKE.

BUT BLUNDERBOAR'S RIGHT ABOUT ME—I'M...I'M JUST A LOW-DOWN CRIMINAL WITH A CHRONIC CASE OF BAD LUCK, AND IF YOU WANT NOTHING TO DO WITH ME, I'LL UNDERSTAND.

HOLD STILL, YOU SLIPPERY PIXIE!

OW! SHE BIT ME!

113

BUT IF THE GOOD GUYS ARE GOING TO WIN, WE NEED THE PLAN, JACK. SO COME ON, LET'S GO MAKE IT HAPPEN.

Make it happen. Make it happen.

A perfect scheme really is all about having the right mark...

For the first time in my life, everything was exactly right.

...and the right team.

So, Plan B...

THAT'S IT! FINE! YOU WIN! I TURN MYSELF IN. I KILLED ONE OF YOUR GIANTS, AND I SHOULD PAY FOR IT.

GOTCHA!

WHOA!

FASCINATING.

BUT I DON'T CARE ABOUT THAT STUPID FOOL WHO FELL OFF THE BEANSTALK. THE ONLY REASON YOU'RE STILL BREATHING IS BECAUSE I WANT MY GOOSE BACK.

SO YOU CAN COOK HER? NO CHANCE. SHE LAID A FEW GOLD EGGS FOR ME AND THEN GAVE UP THE MAGIC STUFF. NOW HER EGGS JUST MAKE HALF-DECENT OMELETS.

I HAVE ALL THE GOLD ONES IN MY BAG.

PRUDENCE DIDN'T KNOW, BUT THE REAL REASON I CAME WAS TO GIVE YOU THE GOLD SO YOU'D LET MY MOTHER GO.

116

click

THEY'RE YOURS, BLUNDERBOAR, SO LONG AS YOU AGREE TO GIVE MY MOTHER THIS BUILDING AFTER SHYPORT TURNS YOU OUT.

OH BY ALL MEANS! I AGREE! THE VERY MOMENT I'M RUN OFF!

FEH! YOU REALLY ARE A FOOL, AND YOUR WINGED FRIEND NEARLY HAD ME CONVINCED THAT YOU WERE CLEVER.

AH, IT'S JUST AS WELL. THE STUPID GO DOWN THE GULLET MUCH EASIER.

ARE YOU GOING TO KILL ME NOW, BLUNDERBOAR? GRIND MY BONES INTO BREAD AND ALL THAT?

A DIET OF HUMAN BONES DOES WORK WONDERS FOR A GIANT'S STRENGTH, THAT'S TRUE, BUT SIMPLY KILL YOU? NO. I'M THINKING I'LL GNAW YOU TO DEATH FIRST, LIKE WE USED TO DO IN THE OLD WORLD.

I'M NOT IMMUNE TO NOSTALGIA.

SO ALL THIS ANT PEOPLE STUFF STARTED TO COVER UP YOUR MURDERS? YOU AND YOUR LOT HAVE JUST BEEN KILLING PEOPLE FOR THEIR BONES.

HMM, HOW SMALL-MINDED OF YOU.

THE BONES WERE SIMPLY AN ADDED BONUS. FIRST AND FOREMOST, I AM A BUSINESSMAN.

117

118

IF THAT'S WHAT—

THAT CURSED BROWNIE SCREAM. WHAT SET THEM OFF?

IT'S A MOB OF PEOPLE. THEY'RE...UH... THEY'RE THROWING ROCKS.

DON'T RUN AWAY FROM A LITTLE SCREAM! THAT'S MY NEPHEW JACKIE UP THERE TELLING BLUNDERBOAR WHAT'S WHAT. KEEP THOSE ROCKS COMING!

DON'T REEL IN THE BROWNIES YET. WE NEED TO KEEP THAT MOB BACK.

BUT WHY ARE THEY—

OOH, I MIGHT HAVE ACCIDENTALLY TURNED ON YOUR LITTLE MACHINE HERE.

IT LOOKS LIKE THE WHOLE "WRETCHED CITY" HEARD YOUR "PATHETIC PEOPLE" SPEECH.

HA-HA! THAT'LL DO IT!

GRRRRRRRRRRRRRRRRRRR

ARGH!

eeeeeeeeee

DON'T TOUCH HIM! DON'T TOUCH MY BOY!

LET ME OUT. I CAN STOP THOSE BROWNIES SO THE MOB CAN GET PAST.

FAT CHANCE.

PLEASE! I MADE A MISTAKE. I WANT TO SEE BLUNDERBOAR SQUIRM.

YOU'VE GOT TEN SECONDS, SPARKLES. MESS UP AGAIN, AND I FEED YOU TO A CAT.

KRASH

EEEEEEEEEEEEEEEEEEE

CRASH

PIXIE SISTERS, GIVE THOSE BROWNIES SOMETHING TO SCREAM ABOUT!

IS THAT PRUDENCE UP THERE?

UHHH...

THEY GOT PRUDENCE!

COME ON, GIRLS!

123

124

NO YOU
DON'T...

RAPUNZEL!

LEWIS, ATTACK!

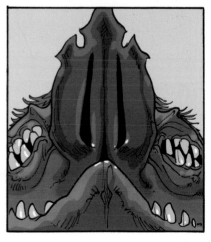

SHLORP

SSSSSSSSS SSSSSSS

GET OFF!

AAAH!

SNRG.

SNRG!

SNRG?

SPIT

SPLURT

SPIT

SSSS SSSSSS

SPLAT

SSSSS

AAAAAAAAAAAA

THUD!

WE GOTTA...
WE GOTTA...

FREDDIE, TELL ME YOU'RE WEARING IT. TELL ME YOU BROUGHT THAT STUPID CATAPULT BACKPACK.

BINGO! STRAP ON, VALIANT LEADER.

OH BOY.

LISTEN... THANKS.

GO SAVE YOUR LADY, MY HEROIC FRIEND. SHE IS WORTH KEEPING, I'D SAY.

YOU GOT THAT RIGHT.

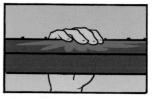

128

I'M BETTING MY CLEVER SON HAS A PLAN FOR GETTING ME OUT OF THIS TILTING SKY BOAT.

And you know what? I did!

THE BLUNDERBOAR BUILDING, IT'S YOURS NOW, OR WHAT'LL BE LEFT OF IT AFTER THAT MOB CHASES THE GIANTS OUT. BLUNDERBOAR AGREED, YOU HEARD HIM. THE WHOLE CITY HEARD.

UM, BLUNDERBOAR LEFT THESE BEHIND...I DIDN'T THINK IT'D BE STEALING THIS TIME. I FIGURED THEY COULD HELP PAY FOR REPAIRS ON THE BUILDING AND AROUND THE NEIGHBORHOOD...

AND BUY A SHE-GOAT BESIDES, I'D WAGER.

MOMMA, I JUST WANT YOU TO KNOW, I'M DONE WITH THE STEALING AND SCHEMING. FOREVER. I'M ONE OF THE GOOD GUYS.

YES, YOU ARE. YOUR POPPA WOULD BE PROUD.

She touched my cheek and something inside me slid back into place. Something broken didn't hurt anymore.

HERE'S ONE FOR LUCK.

GIVE THAT BRUTE WHAT-FOR FROM YOUR MOMMA!

I heard crashing and figured Rapunzel had found Blunderboar.

She was just out of his reach, and it seemed he wouldn't leave the controls. For the moment.

COME CLOSER SO I CAN SNAP YOUR NECK.

THAT'S SURE A TEMPTING OFFER.

CRASH

INSTEAD,
WHY DON'T YOU LET
ME TAKE THE WHEEL SO
I CAN TIP THIS SHIP OVER
AND SEND YOU SPRAWLING
TO YOUR DOOM?

SNAP

CRAK

Come on, Blunderboar. Leave Rapunzel so you can come out here and murder me.

I'LL GET YOUR SPINE, YOU THIEVING RODENT!

THAT'S NICE. YEP, A WISH A DAY.

I WISHED I COULD FOLLOW YOU, AND I ENDED UP HERE.

DOGGONE IT, I SHOULD HAVE JUST WISHED YOU DEAD.

I'LL SHOW YOU DEAD!

NO, YOU CAN HAVE THIS EGG! JUST LET US GO!

I could see her start to wake...

I had to keep the oaf distracted...

HERE! JUST TAKE IT!

...long enough for her to get into position.

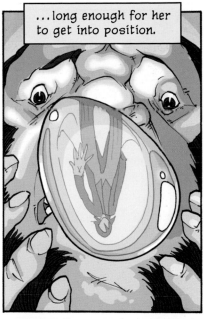

I WISH YOU DEAD.

Not the best of signals, but I knew she'd understand.

My Punzie.

As smart as they come.

IT'S A SHAME HOW YOU JUST CAN'T TRUST MAGIC THESE DAYS.

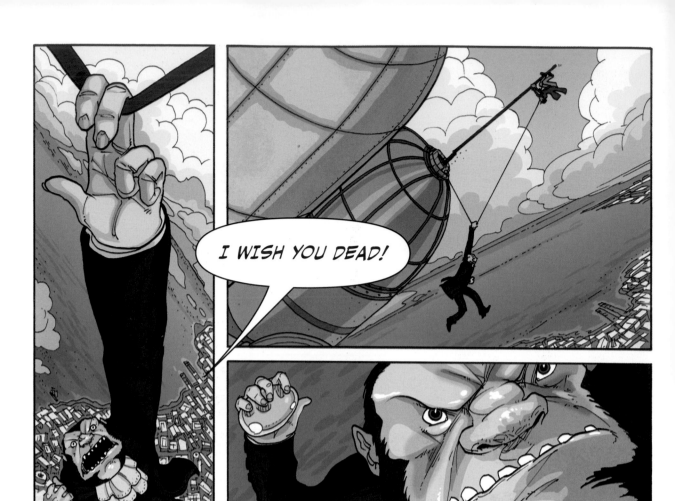

Yet another unforeseen consequence.

But who would've guessed Mr. Frilly Shirt had that kind of pitching arm?

YAAAAAH!

No.

No!

SNAP

YAAAAH!

Lucky Blunderboar weighed so much more than me. The pulley was bringing me up fast.

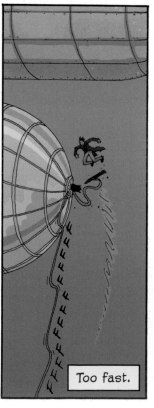

Too fast.

HOLD ON THERE, MISTER.

141

GUESS WE SHOULD FIGURE OUT A WAY TO GET BACK. THERE'S BOUND TO BE LOVELY GIRLS IN THAT ADORING CROWD HOPING TO KISS THE HERO...

AND I GUESS YOU'D LIKE TO LEAP INTO FREDDIE'S ARMS.

FREDDIE?

LISTEN, I DON'T CARE IF HE'S SO RICH HE WIPES WITH PAPER MONEY AND HAS THE WHOLE "HANDSOME" THING GOING ON.

YOU'RE MY GAL, RAPUNZEL, AND I'M NOT JUST GOING TO FALL DOWN WITHOUT A FIGHT, GOT IT?

JACK...

WHAT? WHAT? YOU DON'T THINK I CAN TAKE HIM?

SOMETIMES YOUR HEAD DOES A GOOD IMITATION OF A HARD-BOILED EGG.

SO, YOU DON'T FANCY FREDDIE...

UM...I PICKED UP SOMETHING FOR YOU BACK AT BLUNDERBOAR'S.

IT'S NOT MUCH, BUT PRU SAID...NEVER MIND. NOTHING'S GONE RIGHT. I WAS SUPPOSED TO COME HOME AND BUILD A NEW TENEMENT AND BAKERY...

...AND YOU'D SEE HOW CITIFIED AND SLICK I AM AND, YOU KNOW, ADMIRE ME, MORE OR LESS, 'CAUSE I...I... NEVER MIND, THIS WAS A STUPID—

NO, IT'S NICE, I WANT IT.

THANKS. I...

Tears? Not quite the reaction I'd hoped for.

142

UH, YOU OKAY, PUNZIE?

YES, I JUST— I DIDN'T THINK YOU LIKED ME, YOU KNOW, LIKE THAT, ANYMORE.

THAT'S BECAUSE I'VE BEEN A RIGHT NUMBSKULL.

THAT'S ABOUT THE SWEETEST THING YOU'VE EVER SAID. I HAVE SOMETHING FOR YOU, TOO.

MY POPPA'S... YOU FOUND THIS? BUT WHEN?

YOU GUYS WERE BUSY MAKING THE TRAP, SO I—

HOW DID YOU FIND THE PAWNSHOP?

I LISTENED WHEN YOU TALKED ABOUT IT, FIGURED SOME STUFF OUT, CROSSED MY FINGERS IT WAS STILL THERE. PRETTY GOOD FOR A BACKWATER GAL, HUH?

PRETTY GREAT. THIS IS... THIS IS...